Serenity

Shrava Gupta

Presentation by *BookLeaf Publishing*

Web: www.bookleafpub.com

E-mail: info@bookleafpub.com

ISBN: 9789357744447

First edition 2023

DEDICATION

I would like to dedicate "Serenity" to anyone who is going through hard times... you must always trust your ardent spirit that will ensure that you survive, no matter what.

Learn and value the art and beauty of "starting again."

ACKNOWLEDGEMENT

I must, wholeheartedly, thank my Parents for sometimes believing in me and for their eternal support even in my risky ideas and decisions because of which I am able to live a life that allows me to think freely and imagine profoundly.

My sister, my avid critic, who gives me a reality check from time to time, and allows me to have a more keen insight into humans and life.

Every person who has been in my life for a long or brief; each one of you has left an indelible impact on me.

I now have the clarity to value and cherish the difficult phases of my life, possibly orchestrated by God, that made me strong and filled my heart with humility, and an inquisitive desire to know more.

PREFACE

I wanted to be an author, primarily of short stories, for as long as I remember. I never believed poetry could be my niche or it I could express my ideas or imaginative flare through it. But my perception changed over the years and I came to understand that a poem of few lines could convey more than even a novel could if it was written with the goodness of heart and purity of thoughts.

I am not biased toward any theme, barring nature, but I have created and curated these verses over several years when I was trying to rewrite my own life's story and trying to stand up again. Several global events had unfolded, and my life was also unfolding, though mostly uneventfully; but everything made me think and feel profoundly. I realised the only way to calm the uneasiness in my soul was to put down these quickly dissipating ideas and emotions to go back to them and understand my own mind.

So, here it is... an unfinished canvas of some emotions that made me think and reflect.
I do hope anyone who finds it worthwhile to read this book of verses will be able to relate to

some of them and will find comfort in a few of the words, as they comforted me during my lowest phases of life and gave me the strength to keep moving forward.

The Last Wish

Unsuccessfully...
we chalk out plans for our lives,
being oblivious to its
Arbitrary unpredictability.
I have given up...
On making plans for this world
Rather, I have a perfect vision
for when I do languish.

Incapacitated as I will be,
Obviously...
I would beseech my kindred
to facilitate me in being one with God.
No intention of sullying the Ganges,
Just wish to get absorbed,
Accepted into nature.

Spread my ashes in a forest
I will with the whole heart (and everything)
Nourish the trees,
Enjoy the company of bright birds and bees.
My days will be filled with nature's rhyme,
Nights with its melodies.
My soul will be eternally intoxicated
Without a single drop of wine.
Wild whistling winds will wake me up,

Serene soothing songs slowly will summon
sleep.

What more can I ask for?
It may seem like a hermit's desire
But death cannot douse the heart's fire.
Languishing towards the unseen,
While in quarantine,
Our eyes and minds have been opened,
Finally... as we long for our true abode
Because......

God's in Nature
and Nature is God.

Iceberg

More deep down than high above;
hiding from the world in obscurity.
drifting away from kindred,
a variant of what was bred.
Gratified in its own brevity,
donning aplomb veneer over viscus molotov.

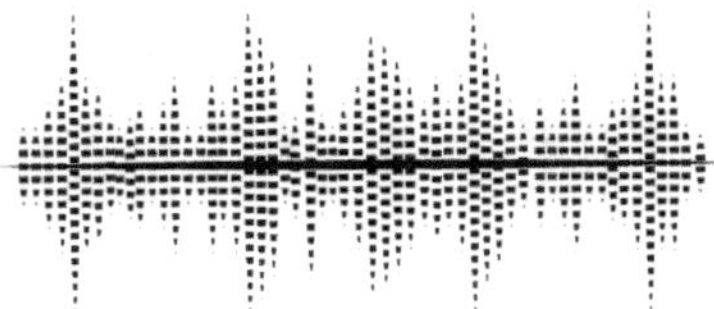

Serene Sorrow

Are clouds lamenting with me?
Did they feel what no one else could see?
Shedding tears of grief is easier
than holding them back.
These pearls of soul convey what words often
lack.

Dear Clouds, do not sing your melody
I can cry myself to sleep...
these infinite sorrows, the heart has to keep.

Earth's escaped breaths...
you can try but won't render comfort
to the heart that is so much hurt.

I do look for solace in your tears,
A few moments of grief may banish all the fears.
Your bright interventions frequently distract me,
But today, I want to wallow in my sorrow, just
let me be.

Free in a Cage

Heart is a free bird a cage can't contain,
having fathomless joy and immense pain.
Once it sets itself onto someone,
The brain has no option but to go numb.
The heart can be obstinate; it wants what it
wants...
Cherished thoughts and images become its
haunt,
It is wise but also reckless,
The brute can create such a mess!

I might let it have its way
the truth is... I have no say...!

Unsaid and Unrequited

Things left unsaid say more,
Often than the words which touch the shore.
Do we say what is in our heart,
And risk for things to fall apart...?
Is it better to share our thoughts and feelings,
To let the overflow of emotions, stop the
reeling...?

Time and age with their cruel indifference
Don't leave a niche for inference.
Do we pour out our heart,
Or remain silent like art?

UnConflicting Perspectives

I may see six, while you see nine,
some may even see sixty-nine.
But I shall respect your perspective
if you are open to understanding mine.

United by beginnings, and divided by opinion,
there is plenty of space for relevant oblivion.
Birthed the same,
let's not die in vain.

Blessed with the liberty of life and thought,
Humans keep tabs on the scores of wars we
fought.
God's perfect creation...
is heading for annihilation.

We are too blind,
not from the eyes but the mind,
to see a simple reality -
Humans are made of love and for love,
there's no paucity.

The divine mantra is to open our hearts
for love and respect for the differences
that unite us though they keep us apart.

So, I will see from your sight,
while you see from mine,
It will be the path to make the world divine.

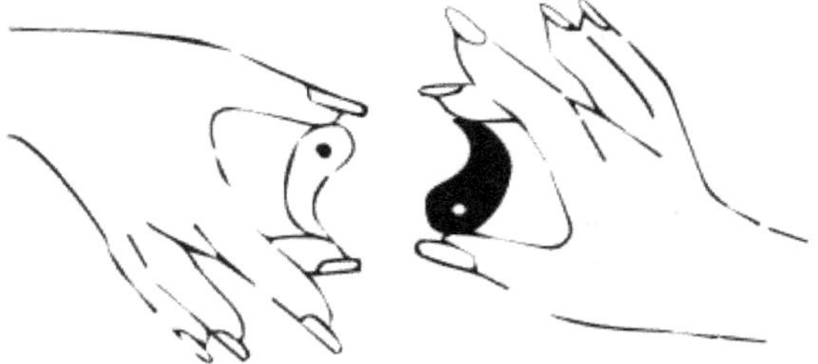

Tainted Trust

I have learned not to trust people,
this sin causes immense trouble.
Though the heart is fickle
but the mind has its flaws,
the source of irrationals emotions,
love cannot be fettered with laws.

We all are guilty of trusting the words
and loving the vile veneer.
Even the wittiest of birds
are foolish and easy to ensnare.

I am and will be an optimist
still, the hurt heart ponders
over the opportunities missed.
Though I have learned a bitter lesson,
don't know how this ache will lessen

Maybe everything is meant to be
but we all are just too naive to see.

Grey

Though it may seem sans colour,
But grey is anything but lacklustre.
From the hue of primordial cloud
To the ashes of humble and proud,
Everything and everyone is grey.

Though overlooked often,
Grey invokes the vibes that soften
The extremities of passion and emotion.

An achromatic 'colour'
Grey is neither material nor spiritual.
An undefined hue,
Defines the humans through and through
It is the colour of the pure human psyche;
None is as good as white
Nor as nefarious as black or spikey.
Grey is ubiquitous, yet out of sight...!

Grey Matter, the source of wisdom and intellect,
A tint from which emotionless indifference
reflect'.

A conduit between white and black,
It is the colour of the paths we track.
Sophisticated yet dull,

Grey remains modest and subtle.
Though there is not much to say,
But "the color of truth is grey."

Souls' Fleeting Love

Today I am all yours
and you are mine...
It took an eternity for love of ours
To free itself and savour this time.

We waited for an eternity to find each other
Let's not while away precious moment...
Our burning hearts with souls of feather
Seek to rescue each other from this torment.

Sweet wine, music is of no need
Our ancient love is burnt deep into the flesh.
Soul, a soothing fiery seed,
And our minds together a mesh.

Savouring these moments as infinite
Flowing through the silky fibers of time...
Our love shall end tonight

"Friends" and a Foe

The Eagle perched atop its ivory tower
while the Bear mauled the Nightingale
in a naked show of power.

The massacre began when other Beastly
Animals
let the Hedgehogs cajole the Nightingale
to prick the Bear, fanning its old fiery glorious
tale.

As the entire Watch watched their nest get
annihilated,
the Eagle and the Hedgehogs kept the hell-fire
burning
while the vicious Bear was effusively hated.

The naive Nightingale sang the hopeless song,
beseeching its allies, knowing it didn't have
long.
The almighty Bear was ready to kill or maim
the Nightingale;
the entire jungle wickedly watched this
cautionary tale.

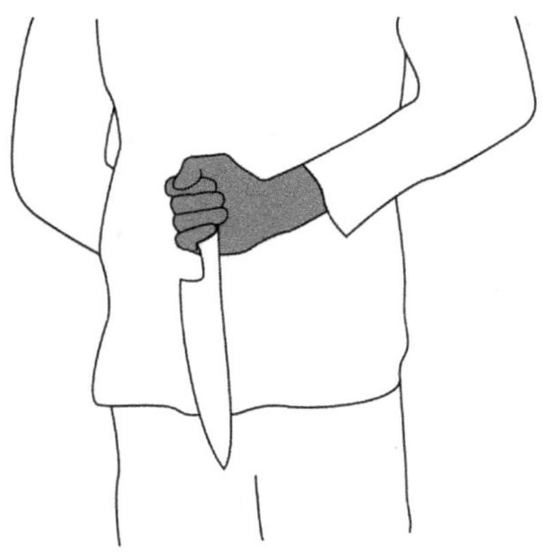

The War

For the war created by other'
I was inveigled to leave my mother...
A crescendo of gloom and fear overtook
vogue and valor in a million crimson brook.

Ceasing all the soul's affectations,
I went after newfound affections...
Promising to return to the beloved,
the entire troop to doom was led.

The confluence of the enemies on the field
gave wounds that can never be healed.
Fighting the wars of someone else,
each warrior fell with the tolling bells.

Those who were languishing with it,
saw their souls escape the cage bit by bit.
The fireworks around them...
pushed the debris away from life's hem.

With the last few borrowed beats,
disavowed the pain in the loaf of meat.
Now...understanding the futility of war,
yearning to live grew even more.

The brave and wise mighty men
designed the battles to defend
their nation and the men
with our ardent spirits and their regal pen.

For the wars created by others...
The precious sons were taken from their
mothers.

Healing through Pain

Drowning in the deep dark space,
Hollow... lingering sorrow
Cold, unfeeling, undefined suffering
A constant desire to escape.

Escaping the world, evading life
Being engulfed by it is a losing fight.
It can manifest itself in a gory glory
Or stays hidden in plain sight.

Sad faces or happy facades,
It can reside in anyone's heart.
A quicksand that slowly swallows its prey
Merely being alive is a struggle each day.

Only you know its pain without feeling it...
Yet fighting this demon with hope and optimism
Is an essential journey to reclaim your soul bit
by bit.
Wield the sword and slay the demon,
Falling into a dark dungeon may be inevitable
But courage to get out is the essence of being a
human.

Spring

Earth is thawing after lifeless winter
As new life springs from melting snowy glitter.
Nature is enriched with a myriad of colours
And sweet melodies of birds with tinted
feathers.

Fragrance of blooming flowers and intoxicated
breeze
Accompany the gentle wind blowing through
trees.

Period of rebirth and rejuvenation
Is the best phase to get out of hibernation.
Filled with hope and light,
Gives the strength to win another fight.

Go out, feel the gentle sunshine...
If yesterday was lost, today you'll be fine.

Kintsugi

Flaws and cracks are precious,
Adding the essence of uniqueness,
Ridding people of anything affectatious.

Damages in life can be repaired and dealt with,
Lessons learned through struggles are gilded.
Accepting flaws is quintessential to life,
The essential path, far from strife.

Before others... showing yourself love
Is the essence of true strength
To direct life's path up and above.

Time is transient and life sublime,
Attaining perfection is a futile rhyme.
So, let those flawless flaws be
Your won battles for others to see.

Undefined

Do you ever look at the stars
Wondering what lies afar?
Those mysterious giants of gas and dust,
Fill the mind with wanderlust.

Science does define the cosmos,
With ever-dynamic theories to propose.
Or is this the work of a Divine Strategy,
Lining the heavenly bodies in syzygy?

Unsure about the present dimension,
Mysteries of black holes or time dilation.
Oh, the arrogance of feeling special,
In a multiverse that is exponential.

Are we the blessed creatures living in heavenly
manifestation?
Or are the pawns being played in a simulation?

An Ode to Our Furry Friends

During those moments of hopeless darkness
The warmth of silent caress,
Can be the gentle medicine
More potent than being with the kin.
That scaly skin or pointy whisker
Can never fail to evoke a snicker.
A silent judge with a mysterious soul
Will always be there to make our lives whole.
Always craving food but love-hungry,
They stick around through heartbreaks or being
angry.
The epitome of love, friendship, and loyalty,
They are the perfect creatures of divinity.
Oblivious to wealth or affectation,
These marvelous monsters crave affection.

Their life begins and ends in a blink of an eye,
Leaving behind beautiful memorable moments
that never die.

Small Talk

Why do we need to waste our breath on small
talk,
When we can just cherish our silent walk.
Each forced word of niceties,
Often is and remains shallow and empty.

Why not instead indulge in the silence,
Walk or sit absorbing the vibes of ambience?
Cherish that cup of sweet warmth
Or read a tale to pass the time of a sloth.

We may know each other
Or be complete strangers, doesn't matter,
But the energy lost in 'small talk'
Won't be retrieved, why indulge in this fault?

So let's acknowledge and spend a few moments
being nice,
But let the small talk not become our vice.

You enjoy your company as I enjoy mine,
Sitting alone and cherishing the present moment
is the best use of our time.

Value your Voice

Your words matter!
Knowing is the beginning of something great,
Profound, honest words can evoke love or deep
hate
But this is not the reason to stay silent,
The storms created by unsaid words turn
violent.

Have the strength to express yourself,
No one else is responsible for your words and
mind,
If the enlightened never spoke up,
The world would have remained blind.

The catharsis of free and honest expression,
The strength of opening your heart is a true
passion.

Promise yourself, know that you deserve
To value your voice and be heard,
Let the ideas and emotions unreserve.

The Eternal Battle

Heart and mind remain in an eternal battle,
One uses emotional tools,
The other rational weapon.
Those who follow the heart the fools,
Though using the mind, nothing different will
happen.

Energised by emotions, memories, and feelings,
The heart misguides through the past reelings.
Mind employs the brightness of thoughts,
And many different wars are as a result fought.

Heart and mind often lack harmony,
This essence of humans is a sworn enemy.
How do we decide who is right,
For whom and on whose side should we fight?

Maybe let them indulge in a duel,
Give both a fight and a reason for fuel.
In the end, whichever survives,
We'll be the ones to thrive.

Soul

Oh, the primordial seed of life,
The mystery unsolved,
The Divine Spark of genesis,
What secrets do you hold?

Are you the pure form of energy
Holding endless beginning and infinite in
synergy?
Are you the essence of the Creation of the
Creator
Or a simulation or a plot being played in a
theatre?

Do you reside in the sentient?
Or even in the lesser variants?
What is your shape or form,
How do you even persist in a storm?

Can life exist and thrive
If you are not there to drive
The organic vessel that is transient
Having profound emotions and ideas brilliant?

An essence of Divine
Laden with cosmic wine,
You remain a mystery to be resolved,
Kindling the spark of life, as immortal tales are
told.

Serenity

Sweet song of soul sung through eternity,
Every mind is filled with this thought...
Reeling desire of the naive and literati.
Everlasting desire to escape the eternal pain
Novel thoughts carry forward the old flame.
It wholly combines water, fire, earth, akash, air
To assist in overcoming the earthly desire;
Yet is a pursuit unattainable by primitive souls.

Savouring a life to be lived harmoniously
Ending in a surreal song that none can wait.
Riveting ecstasy, life's beautiful origami.
Every soul yearns to drown in this ocean,
Nothingness is the epitome of existence.
Intervention supplemented by the Divine Flair.
Toward the souls' eternal home,
Yearning, and pining for serenity are hearts'
prayers.

www.ingramcontent.com/pod-product-compliance
Lightning Source LLC
Chambersburg PA
CBHW070614160726
48003CB00005B/2272